SCHOLASTIC

Fun With Phonics!

Possessives, Contractions, Compound Words & Homophones

by Claire Daniel

SCHOLASTIC
PROFESSIONAL BOOKS

NEW YORK • TORONTO • LONDON • AUCKLAND • SYDNEY

Dear Teacher,

Nothing can be more important in the primary grades than instilling in children the joy of reading and teaching them the skills to become successful, lifelong readers. To do this, we must teach children how to unlock the mysteries of print. Reading instruction that includes systematic and explicit phonics instruction is essential to achieve this goal.

Phonics instruction unlocks the door to understanding sounds and the letters or spelling patterns that represent them. Quality phonics instruction engages children, provides opportunities for them to think about how words work, and offers reading and writing experiences for children to apply their developing skills. The playful, purposeful activities in the *Fun With Phonics!* series offer practice, reinforcement, and assessment of phonics skills. In combination with your daily reading instruction, these activities will help to capture the fun and excitement associated with learning to read.

Enjoy!

Wiley B

Wiley Blevins, Reading Specialist

Cover Design: Vincent Ceci, Liza Charlesworth, and Jaime Lucero
Cover Illustration: Abby Carter
Interior Illustrations: Bill Morrison

Series Development by Brown Publishing Network, Inc.
Editorial: Elinor Chamas
Interior Design and Production: Diana Maloney and Kathy Meisl

Contents

Using "Fun With Phonics"

Fun With Phonics! is a set of hands-on activity resource books that make phonics instruction easy and fun for you and the children in your classroom. Following are some ideas to help you get the most out of *Fun With Phonics!*

Classroom Management

Reproducibles Reproducible pages 7–19 offer a variety of individual and partner activities. Answers or Game Directions appear as necessary in the *Teacher Notes* section on page 29.

Directions You may wish to go over the directions with children and verify that they can identify all picture cues and read any words in the activities before they begin independent work.

Games For partner games, you may want to circulate in order to make sure children understand procedures.

Working with the Poem

A poem on page 6 introduces the phonics elements in this book—compound words, contractions, possessives, and homophones. Start by reading this page aloud to children. You may want to duplicate the poem so children can work with it in a variety of ways:

Personal Response Read the poem aloud, and ask children how it makes them feel. Do they like the sea? Would they enjoy sailing toward a new land?

Phonemic Awareness Read the poem aloud and have children raise their hands when they hear a contraction. Repeat for possessives and compound words. Then ask them to listen for homophones—two words that sound alike but have different meanings.

Sound to Letter Write the poem on chart paper or on the chalkboard. Have children circle compound words, underline possessives and contractions, and draw rectangles around homophones.

Innovation Talk about how the poem would change if the word *sea* was replaced in the second line. Ask children to make up a new version of the poem.

Connecting School and Home

The Family Letter on page 5 can be sent home to encourage families to reinforce what children are learning. Children will also enjoy sharing the Take-Home Book on pages 21–22. You can cut and fold these booklets ahead of time, or invite children to participate in the process. You might also mount the pages on heavier stock so you can place the Take-Home Book in your classroom library.

Word/Picture Card Sets

Pages 30–31 of this book contain matching sets of Word/Picture Cards drawn from the vocabulary presented in this book. You might mount these on heavier stock as a classroom resource. You might also duplicate and distribute them to children for use in matching and sorting activities. Each child can use a large envelope to store the cards. Each title in the *Fun with Phonics!* series contains a new set of thirty-two cards.

Assessment

Page 20, Show What You Know, provides children with targeted practice in standardized test-taking skills, using the content presented in this book in the assessment items. The Observation Checklist on page 32 gives you an informal assessment tool.

Dear Family,

In school your child is learning about compound words, contractions, possessives, and homophones.

A compound word is a word formed from two shorter words. Some compound words are *football, mailbox,* and *pancakes.*

A contraction is a short way to write two words. It has an apostrophe.

> *I + have = I've*

A possessive shows ownership. It usually has an apostrophe.

> *the bike that belongs to Bob = Bob's bike*

Homophones are words that sound alike but are spelled differently. Some homophone pairs are *knight/night, two/too,* and *sent/cent.*

You may enjoy sharing some or all of the following activities with your child:

Homophone Sentences

Say a homophone and use it in a sentence. Then challenge your child to say a word that sounds the same and use it in a sentence. Use homophones like *one/won* or *right/write.*

Read Comic Strips

Read a comic strip with your child. Then look in the strip for possessives and contractions. Have your child circle them and tell what each word stands for.

Reading Together

To practice reading compound words, contractions, possessives, and homophones, look over your child's Take-Home Book, "Playing With Baby." Ask your child to point out examples of all these phonics elements. You may also wish to look for these books in your local library:

Sincerely,

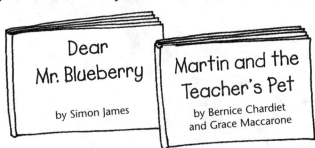

Name _____

Sail Away

Wouldn't it be fun
To see the sea?
In the afternoon sunshine
We could sail free!
We'd use my friend's sailboat,
It's made to take two.
We'd explore a new land
That no one ever knew!

Possessives, Contractions, Compound Words & Homophones

Name _____

Picture This!

Look at each picture below. Say the picture name. Find two pictures whose names together make the word. Cut them out and paste them in the boxes. Write each word.

1. 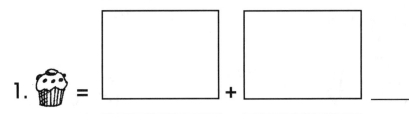 = [ ] + [ ] _____

2.  = [ ] + [ ] _____

3.  = [ ] + [ ] _____

4. 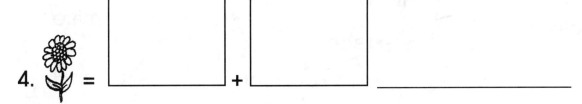 = [ ] + [ ] _____

Now draw and name a funny compound word of your own.

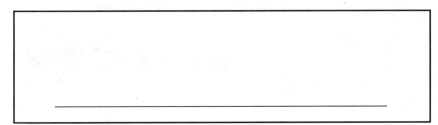

Name _____

What Is It?

Read the words in the picture below. Draw a line to connect each compound word. What picture do you make? (HINT: The answer is one of the words in the puzzle.)

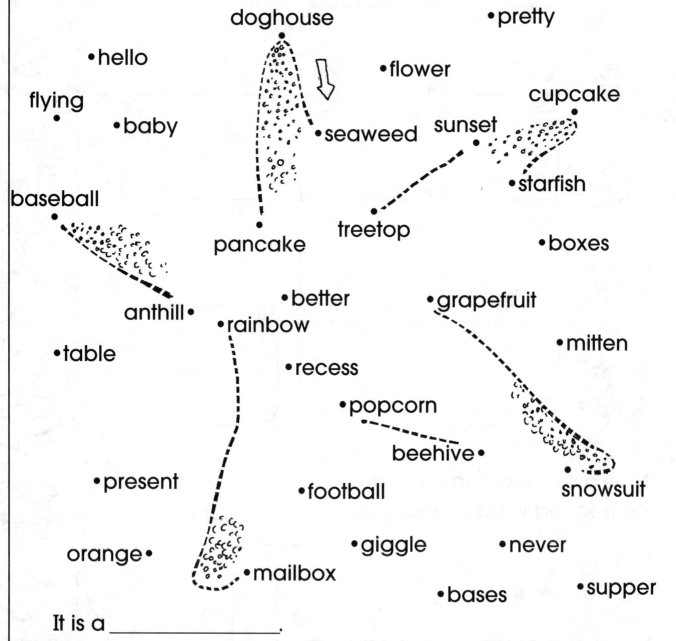

•doghouse •pretty
•hello
•flower
flying •cupcake
•baby •seaweed sunset
•starfish
baseball
treetop •boxes
pancake
•better •grapefruit
anthill• •mitten
•rainbow
•table •recess
•popcorn
beehive•
•present •football snowsuit
•giggle •never
orange• •mailbox
•bases •supper

It is a _____.

Compound Touchdown

Help the team score a touchdown! Write one small word from the box to finish each compound word. Then draw a picture of the object each compound word names.

bow
ball
cup
box
case

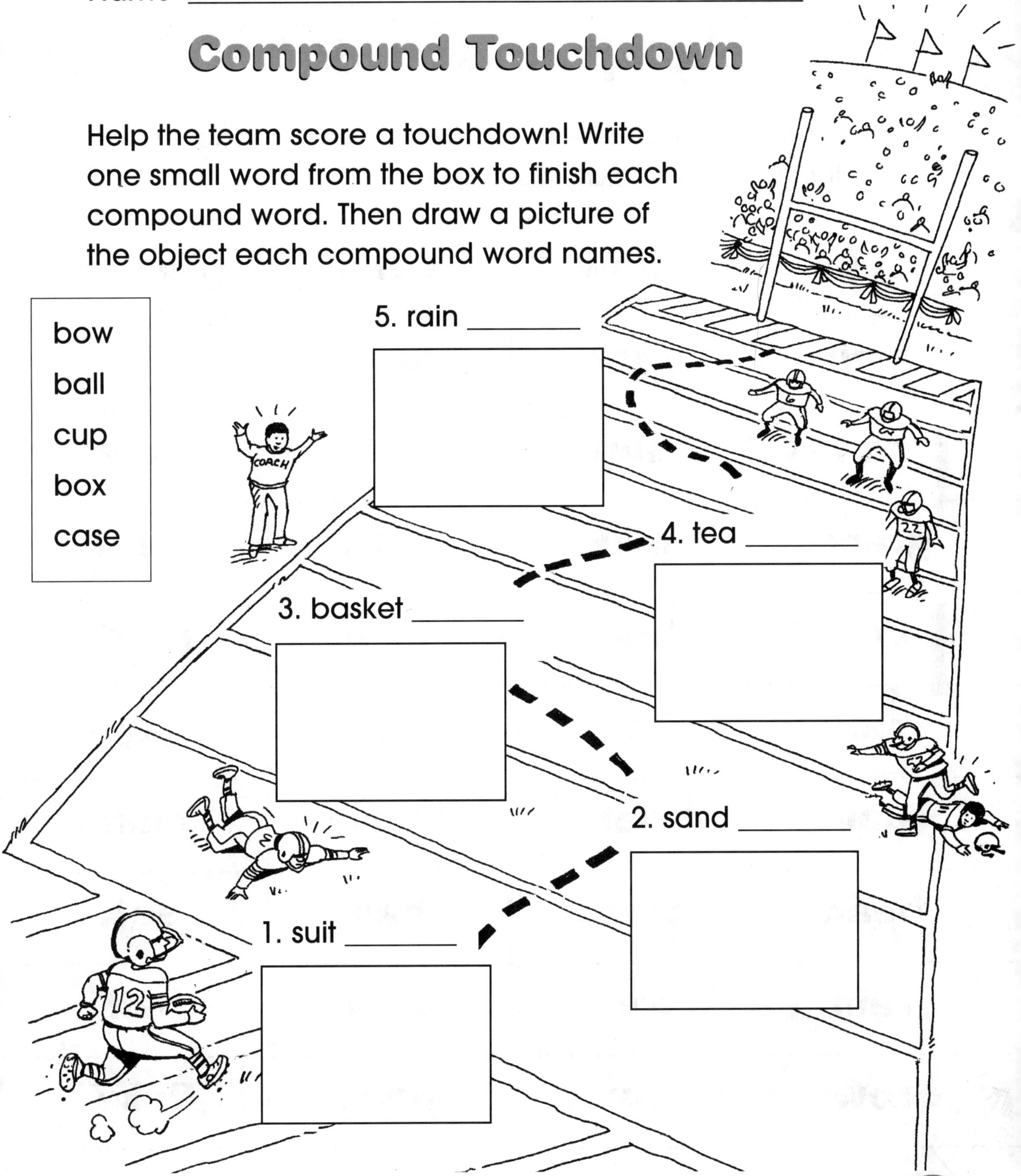

5. rain _____

4. tea _____

3. basket _____

2. sand _____

1. suit _____

Compound Cards

Play this game with one or more friends. Your teacher will tell you how to play this game.

cup	snow	cake	flower
mail	foot	man	top
star	sun	fish	mate
grape	milk	fruit	meal
bee	blue	hive	road
pan	rail	cake	jay
day	oat	dream	man
bean	class	bag	set
rain	tree	bow	ball
row	sun	boat	flake

Name _____

Go, Go, Go!

Hiro and Marie must write contractions to get through the obstacle course. Write contractions from the box to help them.

did not _____

is not _____

have not _____

can not _____

will not _____

do not _____

Name _____

Where's My Hat?

Read the cartoon. Circle the contractions.

Write the contractions for these words:

1. he is _____   2. that is _____

3. it is _____   4. where is _____

5. there is _____   6. what is _____

Name _____

Jumping Contractions

Finish each line of the jump rope rhyme by writing
a contraction from the box.

I have got a penny

_____ got a penny.

He has got a dime.

_____ got a dime.

We have got 11 cents.

_____ got 11 cents.

Jump another time!

Verse Two:

She has got a nickel.   _____ got a nickel.

They have got two dimes.   _____ got two dimes.

Let us jump together.   _____ jump together.

Jump another time!

Contractions With **have, has, us**   13 •••

Possessives, Contractions, Compound Words & Homophones © Scholastic Inc.

Contraction Concentration

I'm	he'll	I'll	she'll
we'll	they're	we're	you're
it'll	they'll	I am	he will
I will	she will	we will	they are
we are	you are	it will	they will

Contractions With **am, will, are**

Name _____

Telephone Talk

Molly and Isabel are talking on the telephone. Read what Molly says. Look at the underlined words. Then write the words as a contraction in Isabel's answer.

We'll	I'm	It's	can't	didn't	you're

Hi! <u>It is</u> 11:30

<u>I am</u> ready to come over

<u>We will</u> ride bikes.

I <u>did not</u> eat lunch yet.

I <u>can not</u> wait to see you.

<u>You are</u> my best friend.

_____ a perfect day.

_____ so glad.

_____ have a chat, too.

I _____, either.

I _____ sit still.

And _____ mine!

Name _____

Whose Hat Is It?

Look at the picture. Color the things named in the box. Check off each thing after you have colored it. Then answer the question.

There is a big hat in the picture.

Whose hat is it? _____

Possessives, Contractions, Compound Words & Homophones © Scholastic Inc.

Name _____

The Picture's Label

Look at the pictures. Read the labels. Cut out each label and paste it on the picture it tells about. Then draw your own picture. Show ownership. Write your own label.

1. 	2. 	3. 
4. 	5. 	6. 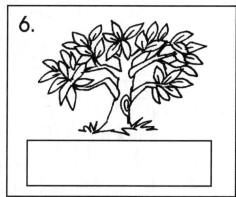

7.

_____

Nilda's doll

frog's hat

tree's leaves

dog's bone

man's suitcase

bird's worm

Name _____

Sound-Alikes

Find the picture words that sound the same but do not mean the same thing. Paste the puzzle pieces together.

hair

son

flour

Flour

toe

pain

tow

hare

sun

pane

flower

What Am I?

Read each riddle. Find the word in the box. Write it on the line. Then connect the dots between each homophone pair. You will see one of the riddle answers!

nose	two	deer	cent

1. I am on your face.
   What am I?

   _____

2. I am an animal.
   What am I?

   _____

3. I am the sum of 1 + 1.
   What am I?

   _____

4. You can spend me.
   What am I?

   _____

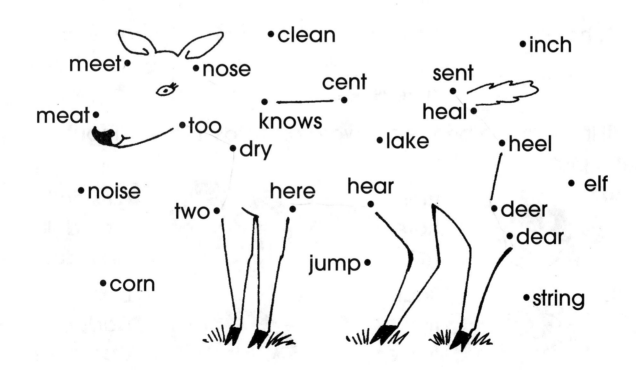

•clean

meet•   •nose   •inch

meat•   cent   sent
                              heal•
        •too   knows
              •dry   •lake   •heel

•noise   here   hear   • elf
    two•   •deer
                                  •dear
                jump•
•corn   •string

Name _____

Show What You Know

Read each word. Fill in the circle next to the word that makes it a compound word.

1. cup
   - ○ top
   - ○ cake
   - ○ coat

3. mail
   - ○ box
   - ○ mill
   - ○ flower

2. back
   - ○ hill
   - ○ man
   - ○ pack

4. snow
   - ○ fish
   - ○ flake
   - ○ bow

Fill in the circle next to the words each contraction stands for.

5. don't
   - ○ do not
   - ○ is not
   - ○ did not

7. she'll
   - ○ he will
   - ○ she will
   - ○ she is

6. here's
   - ○ he has
   - ○ he will
   - ○ here is

8. they're
   - ○ they are
   - ○ they have
   - ○ they will

Fill in the circle beside the word or words that tell about the picture.

9.
   - ○ hair
   - ○ hare
   - ○ hear

11.
   - ○ girls doll
   - ○ girl's doll
   - ○ girls' doll

10.
   - ○ flour
   - ○ fly
   - ○ flower

12.
   - ○ Dad's car
   - ○ Dads car
   - ○ Dads' car

Playing with Baby

Let's play a game.
I'll hide and you try to find me.

1

Okay, Baby. Come find me.
Can you hear me?
Baby?

ZZZZ

4

I can hide under the table.
No. Baby will see me.

Maybe I can fit inside the dog's house.
Uh, oh. It's too small.

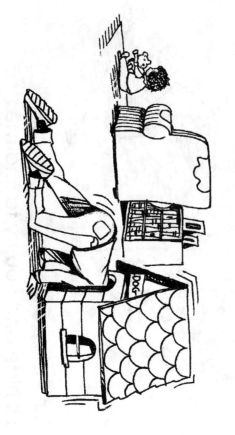

I'll hide here, in back of Mom's chair.
No, she'll see my feet.

I know she won't find me behind this bookcase.
She can't see me now.

Classroom Fun ....

Compound Words, Contractions, Possessives, and Homophones

Tag Up!

Distribute large price labels or tags to children. Have children choose one piece of their own clothing (a shoe, coat, scarf, and so on) and complete the label with their name in possessive form and the name of the item. (For example, *Jacob's shoe* or *Raul's mitten*.) Then help them attach their labels to the objects. Have children put all the items in a box in the middle of the room. Then, one child at a time, have children close their eyes, come to the box with you, and take out one object without looking. Tell them that when they open their eyes, they will look at the label and return the object to its owner.

Compound Art Charades

Divide the class into teams and have the teams take turns playing. Write the following compound words on slips of paper and place them in a can: *starfish, football, inside, raincoat, rowboat, sandbox, frogman, sunflower, mailbox, railroad, oatmeal, classmate, swimsuit, treetop, sunset, anthill, backpack, playpen, baseball, windmill, rainbow, basketball*. Then have one member from the first team choose a compound word from the can and draw a picture to give his or her teammates hints as they try to guess the compound word. Players cannot illustrate the compound word, but they can draw pictures to represent the two words that make up the compound word.

Yours for the Taking!

Small groups of children can sit in a circle, bringing along one item each from their desks. Encourage them to bring unusual things, such as a carrot from their lunchbox, a small doll or toy, a piece of their favorite art, or a spelling test with 100 on it. Have each child show his or her object and place it in the center of the circle. Then begin by saying, "I'm going on a trip, and I'm going to take Sue's spelling test." Have each child in the circle follow you by adding one more thing he or she wants to take that belongs to someone else. For example, the first child might say, "I'm going on a trip, and I'm going to take Sue's spelling test and Mike's plastic spaceman."

Classroom Fun

Find Your Partner!

Whisper a contraction in 10 children's ears and whisper the two words each contraction stands for in another 10 children's ears. (Use the lists on page 29.) Have each child try to find his or her partner—the child who has the matching contraction or pair of words. To search for their partners, children walk around the room quietly saying their words aloud. When children find their partners, have them hold up their hands together. When everyone's hands are up, the game is over.

Bag It!

On paper bags, write the labels *is, am, not, will, are, have, us*. Then write contractions on index cards and place them face down. Have volunteers take turns choosing a card, reading the contraction, and telling what two words each contraction stands for. Then have them place the card in the appropriate bag. Later label three other bags with different words.

Contraction Bingo

Draw a card like the one below, and invite children to play Contraction Bingo. Brainstorm a list of contractions or post a list from the Word bank on page 29. Have children choose 24 contractions to write on their cards in any order. (Make sure they don't repeat any.) Give each child beans or bits of construction paper. Tell children that as you call out two words, they are to find the contraction for the two words and mark it. The first child to get five words across, down, or diagonally wins the game. To verify that the winner has the five words, have him or her call out the contractions and the words they stand for as you check the answers.

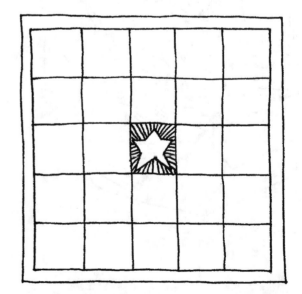

Compound Wheel

Use the pattern on page 28 to make a compound word wheel. Cut out one smaller wheel and one larger wheel, and mount on tagboard or construction board. Place a brad in the center so the top wheel spins easily. Then invite children to play a game with partners or individually. Ask the first child to spin the wheel. When it stops, ask him or her to look for compound words. As he or she finds them, have the child use each word in a sentence to get a point. If there are no matches, the next child tries, and so on. If you would like to make the game noncompetitive, have children work together to get 10 points to win the game.

Chart It Out

Make a chart like the one below on chart paper and have children complete it. Invite children to add to the chart with other compound words they can think of.

Word	Word	Compound Word
sand	box	sandbox
tea	spoon	_____
back	pack	_____
birth	day	_____
leap	frog	_____
_____	_____	_____

Homophone Crossword

Invite pairs of children to choose two words that are homonyms and use them to create a two-word crossword puzzle. For example: *Across: a fruit to eat (pear) Down: it makes two (pair)*. Have pairs exchange puzzles with another pair and solve.

p	e	a	r
a			
i			
r			

Homophone Pictionary

Give pairs of children homophones to write and illustrate. Show children examples of dictionary entries that include illustrations and example sentences. Then, invite them to illustrate each word and/or write a sentence using it. Bind their entries together in a class Homophone Pictionary Book. You may want to use the homophone pairs listed in the Word Bank on page 29.

Instant Activities

Grab a Contraction Write contractions on index cards and place them in a bag. Have children take turns choosing a card and telling what words make up the contraction.

Pair Them Up Provide children with a list of homophones. Then, invite them to work with a partner to choose one pair and write a sentence that uses both words. For example: *I can see the blue sea. I felt weak all week.*

Rewrite the Sentence Write sentences on the chalkboard like these: *I do not have time to go. We are leaving now.* Have children erase and then replace the underlined words with contractions.

Line Up, Contractions! Give small groups of children letter cards for letters in contractions, as well as one apostrophe. Have the child with the apostrophe stand in the front of the room. Then, as you call out contractions, have the children who have the letters in each one come to the front of the room. Ask the children to arrange themselves to spell the contraction and hold up their letters.

What's Wrong With This? Using homophones, write sentences on the chalkboard that use the incorrect word, such as the following: *I ate a juicy green pair. Can I have a peace of pie?* on the chalkboard. Invite volunteers to erase and then replace the incorrect word with its homophone.

Compound Equations Write an equation like this on chart paper: *rain + bow = rainbow.* Then, invite volunteers to make other compound equations out of these words: *peanut, starfish, popcorn, suitcase, beehive, weekend, teacup, outside, himself.*

Possessives, Contractions, Compound Words & Homophones © Scholastic Inc.

Who Does It Belong To? Write phrases like these on the chalkboard and invite volunteers to rewrite them using apostrophes: *the book that belongs to Maria (Maria's book), the tie that belongs to Dad (Dad's tie), the leaves that belong to the tree (the tree's leaves).*

Contraction Hunt On butcher paper, write the title *Contraction Hunt*. Then, during the day, have children record contractions on the paper as they find them.

Compound "Sandwiches" Challenge children to fill in the word that forms the second part of one compound word and the first part of another. Write the following on the board:

dog _____ , _____coat (house)
tea_____ , _____ cake (cup)
flower _____ , _____ hole (pot)
chalk _____ , _____ walk (board)

See if children can think of other compound "sandwiches."

Don't Say It! To demonstrate how useful contractions are, tell children that you're going to try to talk for one minute without using any contractions. It's hard to do! Have children "catch" you and write down any contractions you use. (Use a few deliberately.) Then challenge volunteers to try it. Can anyone beat you?

What Did You Say? As you say a list of words like the one below, have children raise their hands when they hear a compound word: *backpack, tackle, handy, handshake, pancake, pantry, snowflake, snowy.*

Compound Wheel Pattern

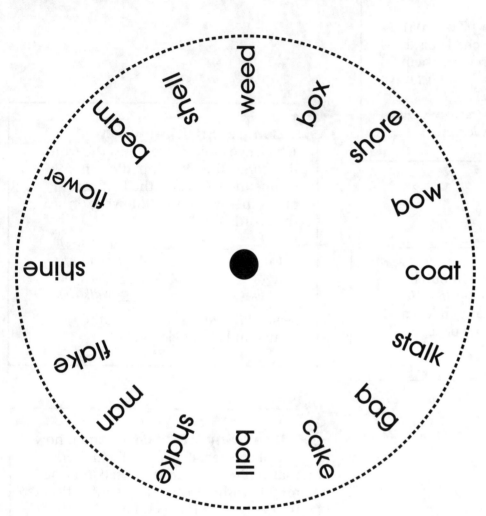

Word Bank

Below is a list of words that you may use to illustrate words with compound words, contractions, possessives, and homophones. Some of these words are included in the Word/Picture Card set on pages 30–31. Ideas for using these cards and additional cards you may create yourself can be found in "Classroom Fun," pages 23–25.

Compound Words, Contractions, Possessives, and Homophones

Compound Words
anthill	peanut
backpack	playpen
baseball	railroad
beanbag	rainbow
beehive	raincoat
classmate	rowboat
cupcake	seaweed
daydream	snowflake
football	starfish
inside	sunset
mailbox	swimsuit
necklace	treetop
pancake	weekend

Contractions With *is*
he's	that's
it's	there's
she's	what's

Contractions With *not*
aren't	don't
can't	hasn't
couldn't	haven't
didn't	won't

Contractions With *have, has, us*
I've	he's
you've	she's
they've	there's
we've	let's

Contractions With *am, will, are*
I'm	you'll
I'll	we'll
he'll	we're
she'll	you're
they'll	they're

Possessives
bird's	dog's
boat's	girl's
boy's	mother's
day's	teacher's

Homophones
beat, beet
cent, sent
flour, flower
for, four
hair, hare
here, hear
meet, meat
nose, knows
pear, pair
peace, piece
see, sea
so, sew
toe, tow
two, to, too
week, weak
weight, wait

Teacher Notes

Page 6 See page 4, "Working with the Poem."

Page 7 *Answers:* 1. cup + cake 2. mail + box 3. star + fish 4. sun + flower; children will invent silly compound words and draw what the word would look like. If children need ideas, suggest "flowerfish" or "suncake."

Page 8 *Answers:* doghouse, seaweed, treetop, sunset, cupcake, starfish, grapefruit, snowsuit, beehive, popcorn, football, mailbox, rainbow, anthill, baseball, pancake, and back to doghouse. *Picture:* starfish; children will write starfish.

Page 9 *Answers:* 1. case 2. box 3. ball 4. cup 5. bow; children will draw pictures of a suitcase, sandbox, basketball, teacup, and rainbow.

Page 10 *Game Directions:* Children can play with partners or in a small group. Have children in each group cut out a set of word cards, mix them up, and place them face down in a pile. Give children five word cards each. Then have them try to match two words that form a compound. If the first player can make a compound word, he or she reads the word, puts the cards down, and takes another turn. If the player cannot form a compound, he or she can ask another player for a card or choose one from the pile. If no word can be formed, play passes to the next child. When any player has no more cards in his or her hand, the game ends and the child with the most compound words wins.

Page 11 *Answers:* didn't, isn't, can't, haven't, won't, don't.

Page 12 *Answers:* Children will circle contractions: Frame 1: Where's, It's; Frame 2: There's, It's; Frame 3: That's, He's; Frame 4: What's, It's. Children will write contractions: 1. he's 2. that's 3. it's 4. where's. 5. there's 6. what's.

Page 13 *Answers:* I've, He's, We've, She's, They've, Let's.

Page 14 *Game Directions:* Children can play with partners or in a small group. Have children cut out the words and place them face down. Then have them take turns turning over two cards at a time, trying to make a match of a contraction and the words it stands for. If they make a match, they keep the two cards. If not, the next player takes a turn. When all the words are turned over, the child with the most cards wins.

Page 15 *Answers:* It's, I'm, We'll, didn't, can't, you're.

Page 16 *Answers:* Children will color and check off Mom's cup, Dad's shovel, the boy's pail, the girl's towel, the girl's shells, the boy's swimsuit, the ocean's waves, the boat's sail. Children will write: Mom's (or Mom's hat).

Page 17 *Answers:* 1. frog's hat 2. man's suitcase 3. Nilda's doll 4. bird's worm 5. dog's bone 6. tree's leaves; children will draw a picture showing ownership and its label with a possessive.

Page 18 *Answers:* 1. hare 2. sun 3. flower 4. tow 5. pane.

Page 19 *Answers:* 1. nose 2. deer 3. two 4. cent.

Page 20 Answers: 1. cake 2. pack 3. box 4. flake 5. do not 6. here is 7. she will 8. they are 9. hair 10. flower 11. girl's doll 12. Dad's car.

Pages 21–22 *Possessives:* Mom's, dog's; *Contractions:* Let's, I'll, she'll, won't, can't, It's; *Compound words:* inside, bookcase; *Homophones:* here, hear; to, too; no, know.

Word Cards

rain	bow	coat	basket
ball	foot	rainbow	raincoat
basketball	football	flour	flower
toe	tow	hair	hare

Picture Cards

Observation Checklist

Writing

- Writes compound words, possessives, and homophones in context

Sound to Letter

- Can distinguish homophones according to spelling and meaning
- Can read compound words and connect their meaning
- Can recognize contractions and possessives in print

Auditory Discrimination

- Identifies contractions in sentences
- Recognizes compound words, possessive, and homophone pairs

Name											

E=Excellent   G=Good   N=Needs Improvement   R=Reteach